This book belongs to

_____

GLITTER
the Tooting Unicorn

By Humor Heals Us

It was a normal rainy day. I was so bored with nothing to do. I couldn't go outside to play. Little did I know that the most magical thing would happen to me.

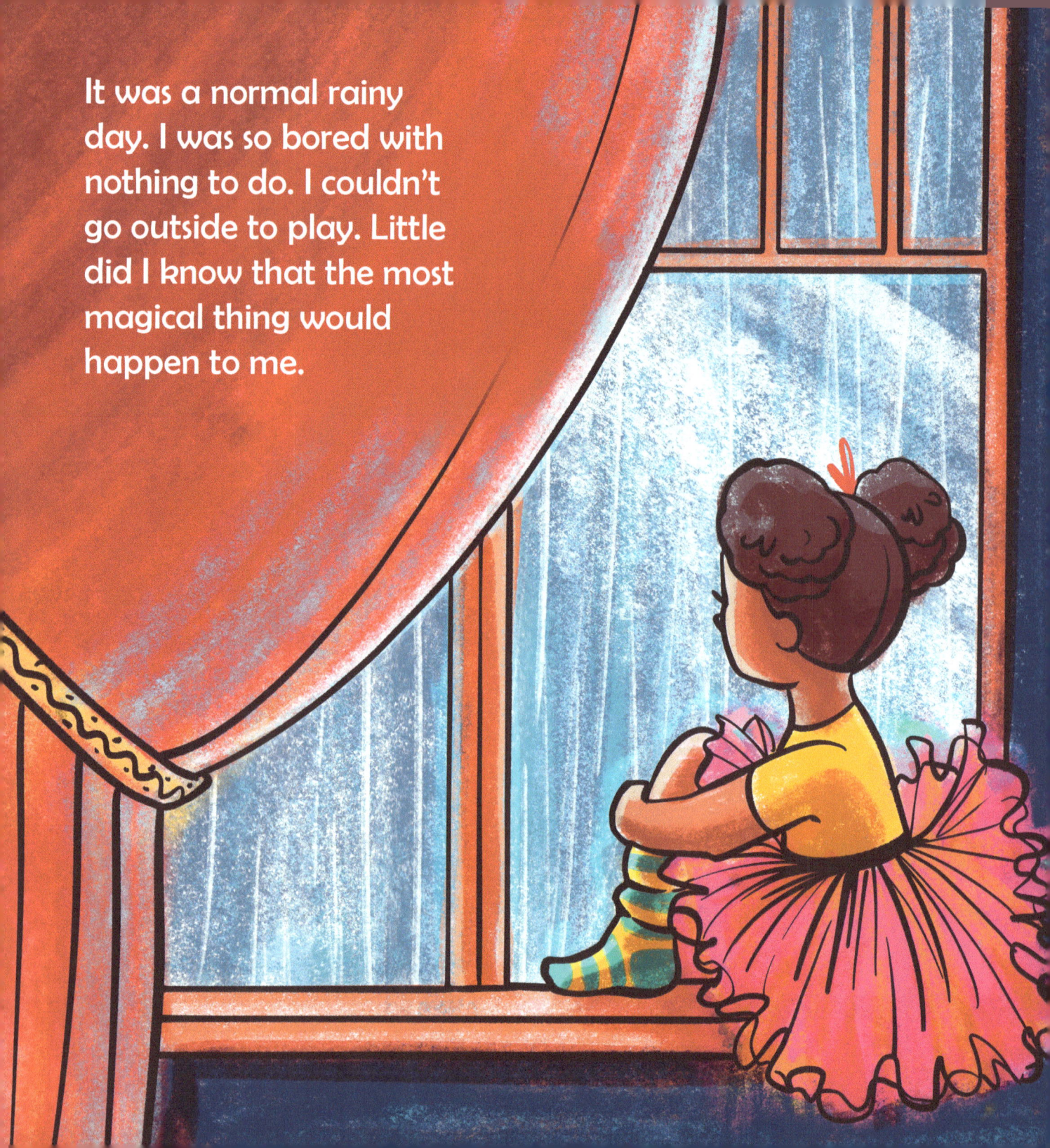

I was trying to count the rain drops. Somewhere around raindrop 482, something sparkly caught my eye.

It was a beautiful, glittery sparkle! What was it?
A diamond? A shiny toy? Or something more magical?

Suddenly, the rain stopped. The clouds parted to shine a light on the super glittery, sparkly thing!

I couldn't believe what I was seeing. It was the most amazing and coolest thing I'd ever seen.

It was a Unicorn!

I raced outside hoping the unicorn would still be there. She introduced herself and said her name was Glitter.

She asked me to go on an adventure. When I asked how, she let out a magical toot that made her fly off the ground like a rocket.

Phewww!!

Before I knew it,
Glitter and I were
high up in the sky!

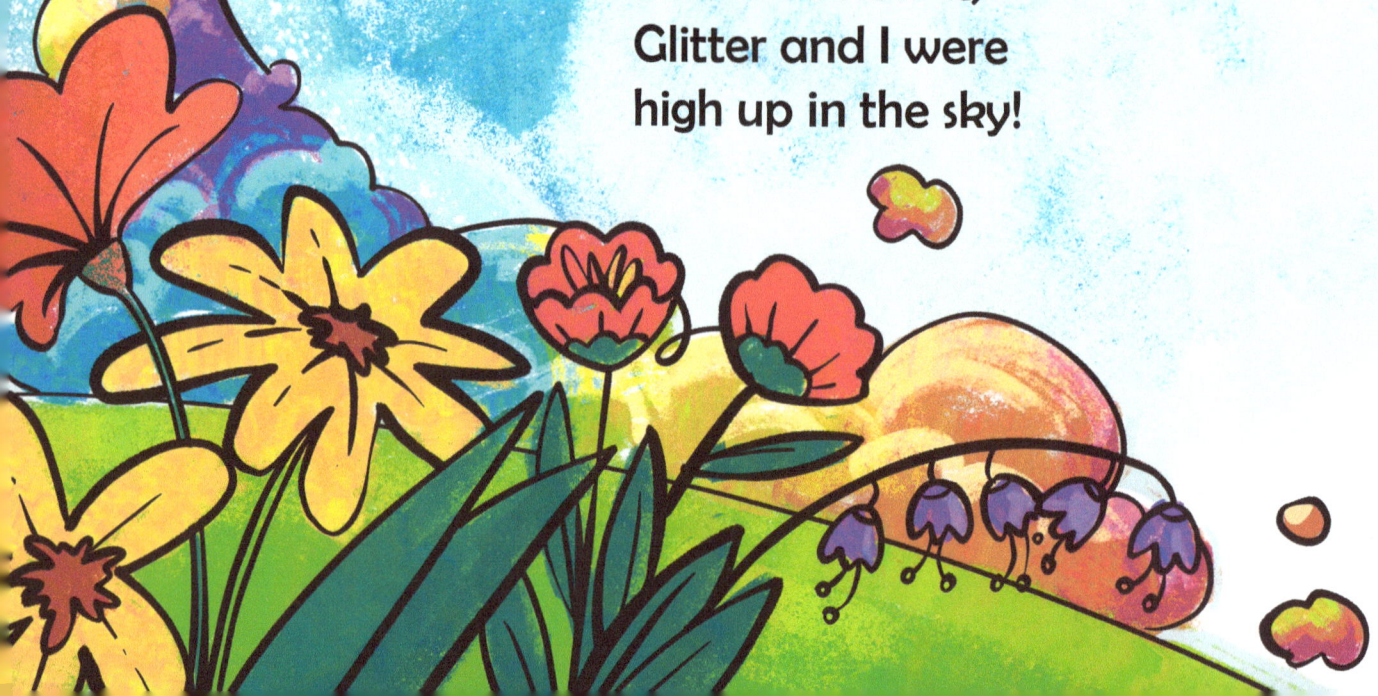

First, we flew to the Candy Orchard where the gingerbread people love to laugh and play.

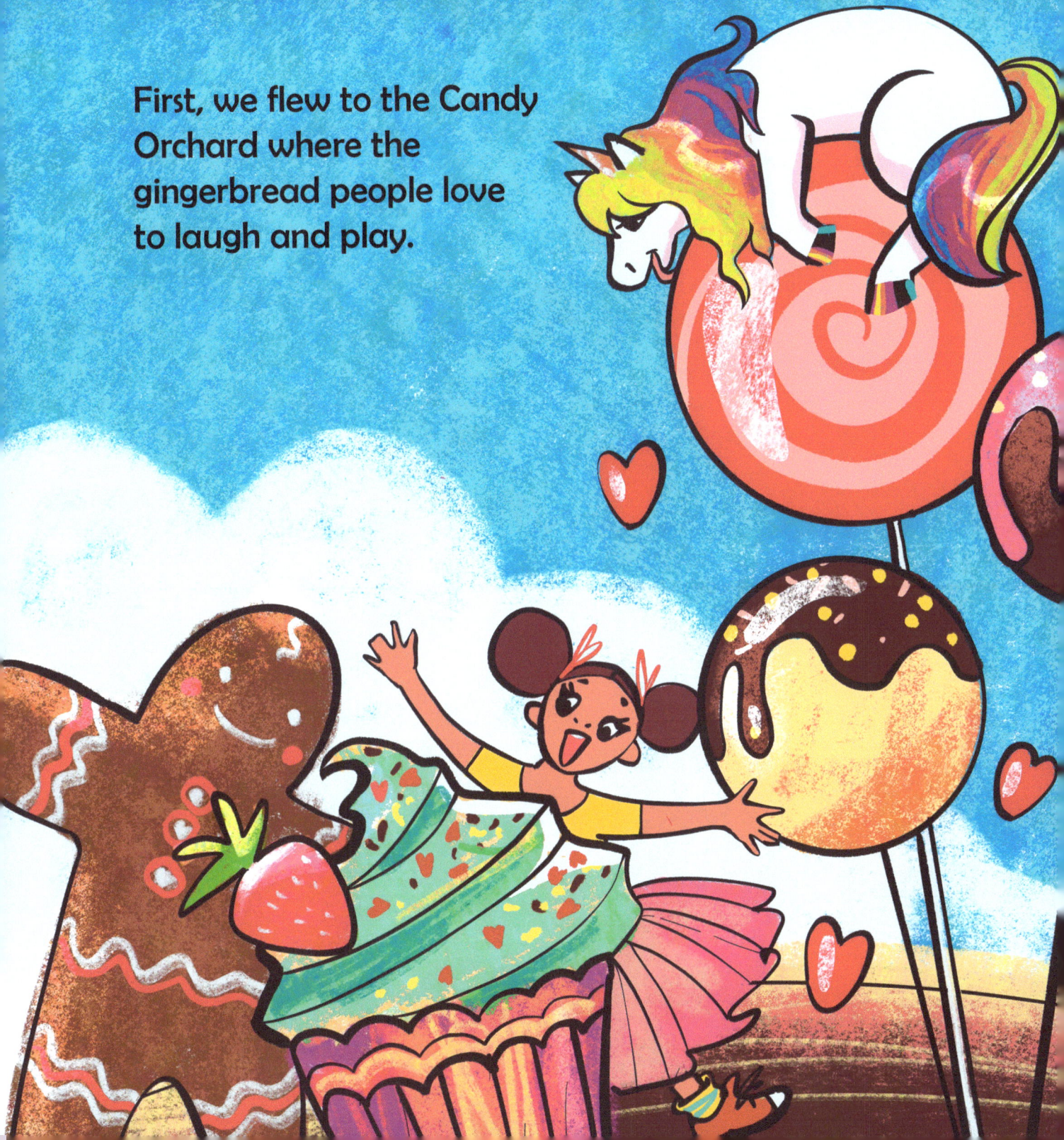

Then, we flew to the ice caves of the north. There we met a gentle Yeti who loved to knit scarves for everyone. The scarves were so soft and warm.

We had so much fun. I hadn't realized how late it had gotten. I didn't want to go home but told Glitter I had to go back.

Fast as we had left, Glitter brought me back home. I couldn't believe how fast those magical toots could take her.

I gave Glitter my scarf to remember me by. I didn't want the day to end, but I knew my parents would be wondering where I was.

Glitter said she would be
back one day, especially if I
believed in the magic. She
said that if I did, the magic
would always be inside me.

I wanted to tell my Mom and Dad about the amazing things I had seen. So, I raced home as fast as I could.

When I told my Mom and Dad about Glitter, I could tell that they thought I was making it up.

I wished Glitter had stayed to show my parents that the magic was real. If only there was a way to prove it to them.

I felt a rumble.

I felt a tumble.

The magic was indeed in me all along!

Follow us on FB and IG @humorhealsus
To vote on new title names and freebies, visit
us at humorhealsus.com for more information.

@humorhealsus   @humorhealsus

www.ingramcontent.com/pod-product-compliance
Lightning Source LLC
Chambersburg PA
CBHW042026090426
42811CB00016B/1758